A *Special Garden*

Heather Hammonds

Contents

Rigby

A Harcourt Achieve Imprint

www.Rigby.com
1-800-531-5015

Our Garden

We have things to see
and things to smell
in our garden.
It is a special
garden.

We have things to hear,
things to feel,
and things to taste
in our garden, too!

3

A Special Garden

You can make a special garden.

You will need:

soil

plants

plant pots

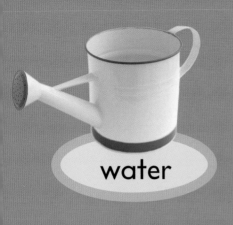

water

two bowls

little stones

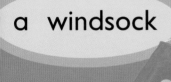

a windsock

wind chimes

Things to See

You can put
lots of things to see
in your garden.

- Put some flower plants
into a pot.

A **windsock** will spin around and around on windy days.

- Put a windsock on a tree branch.

Things to Smell

Some plants smell very good.

- Put a curry plant
  and a lavender plant
  into two pots.

- Put them in your garden.

curry plant

lavender plant

9

Things to Hear

You can put things to hear in your garden.

Wind chimes

make a good sound on windy days.

- Put some wind chimes in a tree.

11

Things to Feel

Little stones feel hard.

- Put some little stones
  in a bowl
  in your garden.

Water feels cool.

- Put some water into a bowl.

- Put the bowl in your garden.

Things to Taste

- Put **strawberry** plants in pots in your garden.

Big red **strawberries** will grow on the plants. Strawberries taste very good!

Glossary

strawberries

wind   chimes

windsock